• ARCHITECTURE & DESIGN LIBRARY •

FORMAL VICTORIAN

• ARCHITECTURE & DESIGN LIBRARY •

FORMAL VICTORIAN

Ellen M. Plante

FRIEDMAN/FAIRFAX
PUBLISHERS

A FRIEDMAN/FAIRFAX BOOK

© 1996 by Michael Friedman Publishing Group, Inc.

Library of Congress Cataloging-in-Publication Data available upon request.

ISBN 1-56799-257-9

Editor: Susan Lauzau
Art Director: Lynne Yeamans
Layout: Joseph Rutt
Photography Editor: Samantha Larrance
Production Associate: Camille Lee

Color separations by Bright Arts Singapore Pte. Ltd.
Printed in Hong Kong and bound in China by Midas Printing Limited

For bulk purchases and special sales, please contact:
Friedman/Fairfax Publishers
Attention: Sales Department
15 West 26th Street
New York, New York 10010
212/685-6610   FAX 212/685-1307

For my sister Ann and with special thanks to my editor, Susan Lauzau,
and the rest of the staff at the Michael Friedman Publishing Group.

Contents

INTRODUCTION

The modern-day revival of Victorian interior design has captured our hearts as well as our imaginations. Taking its cue from a variety of nineteenth-century revival styles and reform, formal Victorian decorating today combines solid comfort and classy good looks with the glamour of the Gilded Age. Stylish enough for gala affairs yet intimate enough for a cozy tea, a formal Victorian decor is also perfect for that special nook where you retreat with a book or the gleaming kitchen where you prepare the family meal. And it's a style that's unsurpassed when it comes to softening the high-tech lines of everyday necessities such as the television, the microwave oven, and the computer.

The Victorian era was designated such in honor of England's Queen Victoria. The years 1837 through 1901 officially mark the period of her reign, but the romance of the nineteenth century and its far-reaching impact on architectural and interior design lingered through the early years of the twentieth century.

During the nineteenth century, interior decoration became increasingly important as a growing middle class acquired the means to create elegant parlors and handsome, almost baronial, dining rooms. It was in these rooms that the Victorians conducted busy social lives, entertaining on a regular basis. Quiet escape, on the other hand, was found in cheerful sitting rooms, distinguished libraries, or cozy bed-rooms. The Industrial Revolution made affordable furniture readily available, along with machine-made wallpapers, carpets, and paints. Household experts stood ready to dispense advice on everything from architectural styles to the latest home fashions, including furniture design, room arrangements, window dressings, decorative accessories, and color choices for walls, ceilings, and floors.

At the start of the Victorian Age, Greek Revival architecture was the predominant style, and rectangular-shaped American Empire furnishings filled the parlors of the aspiring masses and the well-to-do. Eventually, beautiful mass-produced carpets began to replace painted floors or simple floorcloths and factory-made wallpapers opened the door to striking options in interior design.

By mid-century, architects and craftsmen alike were designing homes and furniture with the charm of old Europe. Magnificent Gothic

OPPOSITE: *Simple yet striking, this vignette combines a beautiful banquet lamp (commonly used in the dining room or the parlor during the late Victorian era) with a selection of books and a bouquet of white tulips that echo the color found in the rich marble tabletop. Soft sheers allow daylight to filter in and serve as the perfect window dressing for this formal Victorian setting.*

ABOVE: *While bedrooms during the Victorian era nearly always reflected a feminine taste, the more masculine colors and furnishings of the library have been adapted for this guest room. The rich red—deep colors were favored for masculine rooms—of the carpet is repeated in the bedspread, the trim of the curtains, and the velvet throw that tops the bedside table. A portrait done in oil and a glass-front bookcase decorated with applied gilt medallions are further touches borrowed from the more formal library. Details like the stack of books waiting on the incidental table and the cut-glass carafe and water glass make sure that overnight visitors are supremely comfortable.*

Revival–style homes sported windows and exterior embellishments that arched toward the heavens, and thronelike Gothic Revival–style chairs and settees echoed this same design.

The enthusiasm for revival styles didn't end with the Gothic Revival, however. Picturesque Italianate and, later, Second Empire–style houses were popular until the last quarter of the century and were routinely furnished with delicate Rococo Revival–style pieces or the more ponderous Renaissance Revival furnishings often sold in matching suites. Rich brocades, velvets, and tapestry fabrics began to replace the horsehair used on earlier furniture pieces, creating almost limitless possibilities for color, texture, and design. To provide a fitting backdrop for such lovely furnishings, rooms were enhanced with stunning floral-patterned carpets, windows were lavishly dressed with layers of lace and lovely draperies, and walls displayed color and pattern in wallpapers depicting then-popular landscape scenes, stripes, or subtle architectural features.

Styles have long been subject to change. The Victorian era, marked by rapid industrial growth, booming towns and cities, and increased production of everything from home furnishings to decorative bric-a-brac, was undoubtedly one of the most prolific periods of development in history. As nineteenth-century trendsetters looked to the future, they searched for new expressions of home comforts. The late Victorian era saw houses designed in the embellished Stick Style; the ever-popular Queen Anne Style, with its abundance of decorative elements; and the Shingle Style, aptly named for its shingled exterior.

With these darlings of architecture came myriad new furniture forms and an eclectic array of treatments for home interiors. Reformers promoted a move away from what they considered the excessive interiors of past decades and proposed instead simpler furnishings and wall and floor treatments, and decorative accessories of good quality and craftsmanship.

Eastlake-style furniture—named for Charles Eastlake, the most noted of these reformers—traded the medallions and scrolls that adorned the Renaissance Revival–style pieces of the 1860s for

RIGHT: *The exterior of this Victorian home mixes architectural embellishments like a conical tower and decorative finials with lush greenery and untamed floral beds. The tangle of vegetation softens somewhat the regal lines of the house, offering a subtle touch of whimsy as well.*

LEFT: *Formal Victorian decorating does not necessarily imply rooms filled to overflow. Here the tone is both opulent and spare, achieved with a few well-chosen, elaborately decorative elements. Pilasters with exotic, leafy capitals and impressively complex crown moldings are the perfect backdrop for stunning lace curtains that puddle on the hardwood floor and a nineteenth-century Rococo Revival–style armchair upholstered with a rich, patterned fabric.*

RIGHT: *Careful attention to detail displays quintessential Victorian spirit. A handsome table setting combines elegant etched glassware and fine china with exquisite silver and cutlery. Ornate candlesticks, castor, and antique silver baskets atop a crisp white tablecloth reflect the care that the Victorian hostess took to please her guests.*

smaller, less conspicuous incised lines and geometric patterns. Oriental influence in the form of exotic tasseled and tufted ottomans comfortably coexisted with Eastlake furnishings, and the beauty and warmth of exposed hardwood floors, complemented by sumptuous Oriental area rugs, replaced old-fashioned wall-to-wall carpeting.

New styles in wall treatments were among the most notable changes wrought by the late-Victorian-era reform movements. Entire walls papered or painted in a single color or pattern gave way to dramatic rooms where walls were decorated in a divided, horizontal fashion. Wooden wainscoting, paint, or wallpaper dressed the bottom portion of the wall, commonly called the dado, while the larger midsection, or field, was treated with wallpaper or deep-colored paint such as claret , peacock blue, or rich plum. The very top of the wall, the frieze, was quite often a wallpaper border that accented the color scheme or pattern below.

During the late nineteenth century, Victorians brought their love of nature indoors. In an homage to nature, peacock feathers, seashells, pine cones, and assorted greenery filled the interior of their homes. At the same time, the Aesthetic Movement spawned the popularity of light and airy wicker furnishings that were as appropriate for the parlor as they were for the front porch.

Following closely on the heels of the Aesthetic Movement, stylized flowers and languid swirls adorned wallpapers and tabletop accessories thanks to the penchant for anything Art Nouveau. Even the angular furnishings of the later Arts and Crafts Movement were tempered somewhat by delicate lace curtains and wallpapers with nature-inspired motifs.

Home, to the Victorians, was a peaceful oasis in a confusing, fast-changing world, a center for family life, and a serene setting in which they could entertain dear friends. A century later, the same can be said of our own perception of home. It's no wonder that the Victorian Revival in interior design has been such a success. Timeless in its appeal, formal Victorian decorating today allows us to adopt—and adapt—the best the Victorian Age had to offer in creating our own special haven away from the world.

❖

OPPOSITE: *Myriad fine points create formal elegance, solid good looks, and Victorian comfort in this romantic parlor. Architectural embellishments such as the classically styled fireplace and molded chair rail are hallmarks of nineteenth-century interior design, as are the decorative frieze and stylized floral motif adorning the walls. Such a magnificent background deserves equally lavish appointments: richly patterned fabrics dress the chair and pillows, tiers of lace cascade from windows, and a plush rug echoes the colors of walls and upholstery. A generously stuffed ottoman, turned with buttons and draped with lace, displays the appreciation of the exotic that was so important to cultured Victorians. Sedate oil paintings, mirrors in gilt frames, and accessories of silver and cut crystal add a refined spirit that is pure high style.*

CHAPTER ONE

THE FINE POINTS OF EXTERIOR DECORATION

The past few decades have seen a significant rise in the number of new houses being built to reflect nineteenth-century style, as well as period homes being restored to their original splendor. Victorian architectural designs offer abundant opportunities for decorative effects—outside and inside. Even contemporary homes built in a rather nondescript style are being enhanced with elaborate trimwork, period colors, and spacious porches that reflect the romance of days gone by.

With an eye toward your home's historical style, you can restore, recreate, or add architectural details appropriate to a Victorian theme. Popular shelter publications and specialty books provide abundant information on companies that deal in restoration products and techniques. Customized millwork and gingerbread are likewise available from a number of sources.

Porches, commonly called verandas during the Victorian era, were a typical feature on the majority of architectural styles. Functional as well as beautiful, the porch served to help cool the house, provided a sheltered outdoor area for relaxation and entertainment, and was the ideal display case for potted flowers and ferns. Depending on the particular style of the home, the porch can be dressed with simple or ornate trim, railings, roof brackets, columns or posts, balusters, and fretwork. Even homes designed sans porch can add distinction with a portico—a small, decorative, covered entryway at the front door that often combines columns or posts with a beautiful pediment.

Period-style windows with shutters, decorative lintels (moldings or embellished friezes above the window frames), or art glass panes are yet another way of dressing the exterior of the Victorian home. Windows in various shapes, from arched to rounded to bay, were a favorite feature of Victorian-era architects, and provide exterior adornment that can be enjoyed from indoors as well. Architectural salvage companies, along with noted window manufacturers, are good sources for authentic or recreated windows, trim, and other details, and talented artisans are today creating beautiful art glass or etched glass windows.

Trimwork appeared in various forms throughout the nineteenth century. Improved machinery developed during the mid-Victorian period

OPPOSITE: *A templelike Greek Revival mansion glows in the soft light of dusk. Classical ideals of beauty and proportion influenced this style, which reached its peak of popularity several decades after the discovery of the Parthenon in Athens. Elegant yet simple, the heavy cornices, pediment, and Ionic columns of the portico and second-story balcony pay handsome tribute to the style's Grecian roots.*

allowed for the creation of fanciful wooden ornamentation—commonly called gingerbread—in countless forms. Lace patterns, turned spindles, and geometric designs were popular trimwork used to embellish doors, windows, porches, and gable peaks. Another type of gingerbread popular at the turn of the century was scalloped or "fishscale" shingles used in tandem with square-cut shingles to create a decorative effect on the facade. These too are readily available today at large home building centers and lumberyards.

Other fine points to consider include moldings and brackets used on the exterior of many period homes, roof embellishments such as pointed finials or iron cresting (which has the appearance of a small but ornate fence), and of course, a period color scheme. As the nineteenth century progressed, exterior colors became increasingly decorative as brighter hues and contrasting color schemes came into favor. Larger paint companies have developed lines specifically with the owners of Victorian homes in mind.

RIGHT: *Classical and romantic elements combine in this picturesque facade with Italianate influence. Italianate, or Italian Villa–style, homes took their cue from the farmhouses of Northern Italy, where earthy colors reigned. In reaction to the white houses of earlier decades, which were thought to be too stark and unnatural, proponents of the Italianate style used subtler tones of tan, black, and gray to tie the house to the landscape. The opulent entryway with cast iron corner quoins and lavish trim provides a perfect example of high style Victorian flair. Above the entry is a towerlike bay, which also serves as a second-floor window. Ornate iron fencing and fretwork enclose the covered verandas on either side of the double front door, and eye-catching moldings cap off the second story windows. The overall effect is fanciful but beautiful.*

BELOW: *Conservatories were popular additions to many nineteenth-century homes. This all-season enclosed space is ideal for gardening enthusiasts and serves as the perfect spot for enjoying the outdoors regardless of the weather. Filled with blooming plants and accessorized with iron furnishings reminiscent of the Victorian era, this miniature glass house offers the perfect way to extend your living space.*

ABOVE: *The quintessential architectural fashion of the golden age of Victoriana, Queen Anne style typically combines a multitude of decorative elements for a handsome effect. Here, spindles embellish the entrance and front porch while fish-scale shingles lend ornamentation to the gable. Note the decorative brackets under the eaves and leaded glass window at the third story. Charming, eclectic, and highly decorative, the Queen Anne style pleased the growing numbers of the newly rich, who looked to incorporate symbols of their prosperity into their homes. Today it recaptures for us the true spirit of the Gilded Age.*

LEFT: *A striking example of Gothic Revival–style ornamentation, this home's facade is covered in decorative bargeboards and sports numerous pointed finials. The Gothic Revival took inspiration from the architecture of medieval buildings; pointed-arch windows are a hallmark of this style and the trimwork surrounding the center second-story window achieves this effect, though the windows themselves are standard squares. Luring the eye upward, the design of the iron fence repeats the general patterns found on the building's exterior.*

LEFT: *A splendid example of Second Empire architecture, this home wears the typical mansard roof and incorporates a wonderful tower with arched windows. Often considered the high point of Victorian architecture, this particular style was inspired by many of the buildings constructed in Paris during the mid-century period. Note, too, the decorative brackets under the eaves and heavily corniced windows on the first and second floors.*

BELOW: *Charming Victorian cottages all lined up in a row are a gentle reminder of nineteenth-century lakeside resorts or educational summer chautauquas. Notice how each home is personalized with its own distinctive colors and decorative trim. The front porch plays an important role in these small homes—as it has since the Victorian era—where it serve as an extended living space during the warm months.*

ABOVE: *This beautiful Gothic Revival cottage has the center gable with decorative bargeboard trim, steep roof, and arched window moldings characteristic of this particular style. The roots of Gothic Revival reach back to medieval France and England, where it was especially popular in constructing churches. The highly ornamented veranda is typical, and is furnished with a chair and settee in the same romantic style.*

RIGHT: *Originally built as summer homes for the well-to-do, rambling Shingle Style dwellings were often designed to take advantage of a view. Colonial farmhouses, with their rough and weathered shingles, provided the inspiration for this late-nineteenth-century style. Here, a shingled exterior gives way to a dramatic brick tower with a surrounding porch below. Finally, while many such homes wear natural shingles, the owners of this Shingle Style house have chosen to paint their facade, giving it a more whimsical appearance.*

LEFT: *Exterior details don't necessarily have to be on the facade. This beautiful iron fence holds the outside world at bay while retaining a friendly feeling. Detailed designs in the embellished metalwork set the stage for the grandeur of the Italianate home in the background.*

ABOVE: *This Victorian porch has been treated to architectural embellishment in the form of decorative fretwork. Fanciful curves and swirls contribute an airy feeling that is perfect for the porch, but fretwork was also used indoors, especially at the top of tall doorways or to define quirky nooks and crannies.*

RIGHT: *A close-up of a spectacular porch showcases decorative posts, delicate balusters, and stylized trimwork. Latticework encloses the area beneath the porch and a two-tone scheme in gray-blue and white invites details to shine. Well-trimmed bushes and flowering shrubs encircle the porch for added ornamentation.*

CHAPTER TWO

INTERIOR DETAILS
MAKE THE DIFFERENCE

Regardless of whether you are decorating a nineteenth-century home or a more contemporary space, architectural embellishments are the subtle—or not so subtle—details that can make all the difference when creating a formal Victorian interior. Look to the riches of nineteenth-century architectural details to create a perfect backdrop for elegant furnishings and myriad accessories: vintage windows, warm wood banisters and moldings, old-fashioned hardware, and antique tilework create a comfortable atmosphere and contribute a welcome flavor of the past.

The Victorian Revival in interior design has moved architectural embellishments center stage. The "out with the old, in with the new" mentality that dominated the urban renewal of the 1960s and 1970s has been thankfully traded for preservation, restoration, and recycling. As a result, today we have the opportunity to enhance our formal Victorian decors with relics of the past that recall the romance, craftsmanship, and artistic merit of days gone by.

The beauty of leaded glass panes or an etched glass window presiding over the dining room or parlor reminds us of the extraordinary care Victorians took with the rooms intended for company. But even foyers and stairway landings were treated to stunning art glass windows that cast rainbows of color across glossy floors. Art glass could even be made to imitate thinly sliced agates or marbles.

Admire, too, the gleaming woodwork that was everywhere apparent in the Victorian home. Massive front doors welcomed family and guests alike, and rich wainscoting, sweeping staircases, and decorative hearth mantels add to the grandeur of Victorian homes, then and now.

Even the practical aspects of the Victorian home were dressed to the nines: polished hardware and pristine porcelain fixtures in the bath contributed an elegant touch to a utilitarian space; brass, porcelain, or glass doorknobs in molded or cast designs made art objects out of practical forms; and mundane necessities like floor grates, door hinges, and heat radiators were made lovely with intricate scrollwork and flowing designs.

OPPOSITE: *During the late nineteenth century, the staircase landing became a popular location for a breathtaking window. The beautiful colors and romantic design of this exquisite art-glass window embody the nature-inspired style of Art Nouveau, which infused turn-of-the-century homes with sensuous curves, swirls, and flowers. The window's unusual keyhole shape frames the newel post and is echoed in cutouts on the elaborate stair rail. Lavish woodwork paired with handsome wallpaper and fringed curtains dramatically convey the splendor of the Gilded Age.*

The penchant for detail that pervaded every aspect of Victorian decor is also evident in the exquisite tilework that adorned fireplaces or protected the walls behind massive cookstoves. Even in newer homes or in houses where the original tile has been replaced, the effects of formal Victorian tilework can be replicated using newly laid vintage or reproduction tiles.

Many manufacturers now offer a variety of reproduction windows, woodwork, and hardware that can be easily mail ordered, but don't cheat yourself of the fun of looking for vintage pieces: searching for architectural artifacts is akin to conducting a treasure hunt. Most large cities are home to one or more salvage emporiums, where everything from stone gargoyles to old church pews to garden gates can be found. There has also been an increase in the number of architectural artifacts making their way to large antiques shows. Many antiques shops carry smaller items such as hardware, fretwork, and windows. Auctions and, occasionally, flea markets likewise offer hidden opportunities for a wonderful discovery.

In creating your own formal Victorian interior, you can choose to be practical, following the dictates of design set by household experts of the nineteenth-century, or you can let your imagination run wild, adapting architectural features to suit your fancy. Whether you decide to follow the rules or banish them, let your own sense of design and your delight in the formal interiors of the past guide you to the perfect backdrop for your collection of Victoriana.

OPPOSITE: *Interior doorways accessorized with decorative moldings are a hallmark of Victorian style. Such architectural embellishment adds character to an otherwise plain surface and carries an air of formality throughout the house. Note, too, how the stylized design on the brass door hinge, complete with tiny finials, transforms a piece of hardware into a miniature work of art.*

RIGHT: *Elaborately carved staircases were a favorite of the worldly Victorians. This intricate pattern of interlocking squares and quarter circles, each linked with a turned baluster, is a marvel of artistry. Incised lines, decorative spindles, detailed foliage carvings, and beaded trim combine in a display of nineteenth-century craftsmanship at its most beautiful. Such a high style masterpiece easily stands alone as the focal point of a center hall.*

LEFT: *This high style entryway, with its striking fanlight above the door, matching sidelights, and distinctive cornice molding, establishes at once an aura of almost masculine reserve. The austere, shelflike moldings that dress the doorways on either side of the hall and the simplicity of the beautiful wood staircase further the architectural impact in this spacious front hall.*

RIGHT: *A fireplace can become the focus of attention in the formal Victorian room when dressed with an ornate mantel and overmantel such as this delicately carved example. Dentil molding is set beneath an entablature to form the mantel shelf, while columns— the upper ones terminating in acanthus-leaf capitals—and a broken pediment create distinctive architectural beauty. A brass fireplace fender, a simple screen, the traditional portrait, and select pieces of china atop the mantelpiece are fitting but subtle ornaments that allow the impressive woodwork to command center stage.*

ABOVE: *A decorative ceiling medallion is the perfect backdrop for a vintage hanging light fixture. During the nineteenth century, the ceilings of parlors and dining rooms were commonly adorned with center medallions made of wood, plaster, or papier-mâché. It is this attention to small details that results in the most beautiful rooms.*

RIGHT: *Celebrating the opulence of the Gilded Age, tiers of embellished moldings are reminiscent of a finely decorated wedding cake and draw the eye up toward the ceiling for a visual feast. A rich pier mirror above the fireplace shows in its reflection Gothic-inspired trim above the doorway. Delicately carved stonework on the fireplace and beautiful alabaster vases on the mantel contribute to the architectural impact. This stunning parlor is a perfect example of the way several architectural details work in tandem to create a truly inspiring room.*

LEFT: *Palladian windows were extremely popular during the last few decades of the Victorian era. Here, the window adds architectural embellishment to a combination library/game room. Natural light streaming through the arched window helps soften the somber colors and deep wood tones of this masculine setting. Simple shades on lower windows preserve a sense of privacy; given the Palladian window's location high on the wall, no dressing at all is required.*

ABOVE: *A multitude of details here creates a breathtaking Victorian setting. The elaborate, columned fireplace, topped by a deep porthole window and twin mirrors, is a focal point in the room, but is balanced by the generosity of other features. Art glass windows in subtle amber and gold shades occupy the circular niches on either side of the fireplace, while vibrant turquoise dominates the color scheme of the art glass set above clear panes in the corner alcove. The ceiling has been painstakingly painted to produce a rich effect that sets off the high style furnishings and sumptuous colors of the plush rug below. These decorative elements combine to achieve a formal look that any Victorian would be proud of.*

BELOW: *Leaded glass windows have a heaviness and texture not found in traditional glass. Their weight requires that panes be small and supported by muntins, which crisscross the window in beautiful paths. These particular windows are further decorated with Gothic embellishments that point upward to vibrantly colored art glass panes.*

ABOVE: *This Victorian-inspired bath demonstrates how even the smallest detail can make an immense difference. Gleaming hardware, a beautifully molded pedestal sink, and a claw-foot tub bring elegance and charm to a hardworking space. Outfitted with a comfy chair and dressed wall and ceiling with an enchanting paper, this bath is Victoriana at its best.*

ABOVE: *Indoor plumbing was introduced late in the Victorian era, and since no space for a bathroom had been built into the floor plan, many a homeowner converted a spare bedroom or sitting room into a bath. These roomy baths had space for dressers and armchairs, unlike bathrooms in many modern homes, and benefited from the architectural details that remained from the room's previous incarnation. This spacious bath takes on a formal air, with its beautiful Gothic-inspired windows and gleaming claw-foot tub. Decorative wall sconces flank a framed mirror in an impressive display of good taste, and other appointments—chiefly the upholstered chair and ottoman—add comfort and recall the room's origins.*

OPPOSITE: *Color, texture, and pattern are introduced via the artistic tiles that decorate this lavish mantel; a nature-inspired motif is especially at home in a formal Victorian setting. Beautifully carved wood incorporates geometric forms as well as leaves and the integrated shelf at the side offers further evidence of the ingenuity of nineteenth-century craftsmen.*

RIGHT: *A molded brass door knob with the look of a filigreed piece, complete with a matching backplate, is a purely utilitarian object that has been transformed into an eye-catching detail.*

LEFT: *A decorative wooden chair rail, painted a glossy black, contributes architectural interest to a room; it is joined here by a beautiful wallpaper dado. Note how the colors in the chair echo the hues of the wall behind it but the subtle play of patterns keeps the combination interesting.*

RIGHT: *An elegant cornice and rich moldings help define this formal dining room; its all-white color scheme keeps the look extremely sophisticated. Note the massive pocket doors that separate dining room from drawing room. Guests for a dinner party would traditionally be escorted to the drawing room or the parlor when they arrived; when dinner was served, the handsome pocket doors would be slid back to reveal the splendidly set table.*

CHAPTER THREE
DRESSING WALLS, WINDOWS, FLOORS, AND MORE

F ormal Victorian decorating implies a backdrop that is every bit as sumptuous as the period furnishings and accessories within the room. Walls painted or papered in luscious pastel shades, which gained in popularity with the introduction of gaslights, or in the deep, warm hues that accompanied the reform movements were—and are—key in the decoration of proper Victorian rooms. Well-dressed walls, together with polished hardwood floors or plush carpets; elaborate window treatments of silk, velvet, or lace; and stunning lighting fixtures all work together to achieve a look that is warm yet elegant.

Thanks to the Victorian Revival in interior design, many companies specialize in wallpapers, paints, fabrics, and lighting fixtures that have been designed with the Victorian enthusiast in mind. The difficulty is not in locating sources to fill your needs but in narrowing your choices from the wide range of options available. When selecting wall coverings, window dressings, and floor treatments, consider the particular space you are decorating, the feeling you wish to create, and your own individual tastes and needs.

The Victorians grew quite color conscious as the nineteenth century progressed, and dressing walls in contrasting or harmonizing shades rendered results they greatly admired. Painted walls were often combined with polished wainscoting or, as wallpaper became increasingly popular, with papers in showy floral designs.

Carpeting patterned with floral or foliage designs or with striking geometrics is a hallmark of high Victorian style and is perfect in today's Victorian-inspired room. If hardwood floors are more to your liking, you're not alone. During the late nineteenth century, the Victorians uncovered the beauty of polished wood floors and accented them with lovely Oriental rugs. This, too, is a timeless approach, and works as well in the 1990s as it did in the 1890s.

Windows dressed in layers of fabric—accompanied by elaborate valances, swags, or cornices—are the epitome of formal Victorian style. Ideal for the drawing room, dining room, or parlor, such careful attention to detail adds classic charm. If something a bit simpler is called for, beautiful lace curtains combine delicate designs with unmistakable elegance.

OPPOSITE: *In the nineteenth century, new printing technologies made wallpaper affordable for the middle class, and Victorians responded with enthusiasm. Florals were exceedingly popular, and here are paired with dark, glossy woodwork. Hardwood floors topped with "Turkey carpets," ceilings painted ochre and teal, and luminous art glass windows put the finishing touches on this extravagant hall.*

Ceiling decorations, whether stenciled, painted, or papered, are yet another way of adorning the formal Victorian room, and carefully chosen lighting fixtures put the spotlight on period style.

The Victorian period ushered in so many styles and possibilities with regard to dressing walls, windows, floors, and ceilings that even an authentic period room has the luxury of options when it comes to decorating the shell of a formal Victorian interior.

❖

BELOW: *Handsome wood shutters offer privacy and a touch of architectural embellishment, as lovely lace panels soften the wood tones, filter light, and add a dash of delicate design. The overall effect is simple yet elegant, and is the perfect solution if your preference tends toward pared-down interiors.*

RIGHT: *A fabulous Victorian backdrop is created by combining a beautiful floral wallpaper with an embellished cornice that visually separates wall and ceiling. The opulent hanging fixture has fine details and etched glass globes that make it a focal point in this romantic Victorian setting.*

RIGHT: *Making use of period details creates the perfect setting for classic furnishings and select decorative touches. Stripes adorned with a tiny pattern were a favorite of the Victorians; here, the beautiful wallpaper sets the tone in an elegant, Victorian-inspired bedroom. Layering a stunning area rug atop wall-to-wall carpeting enhances formal elegance and serves to define a special space.*

ABOVE: *Color can be used to create a mood in a room. Here, red tones are stim-ulating and vibrant, playing host to a plush area rug and inviting furnishings. The energy and warmth found in the walls is offset by the cool, glossy white of the fireplace, trim, and ceiling. The entire color scheme is delightfully complemented by the romantic touches found throughout this Victorian-inspired sitting room.*

ABOVE: *Formal Victorian spirit breathes its essence into this richly appointed room. Dark mahogany wainscoting sets off a stylized, foliage-patterned wallpaper and an elegant Oriental rug. Even the ceiling has been treated to rich architectural embellishment in the form of coffered panels.*

BELOW: *High style Victorian flair is immediately conveyed in this stunning floral wallpaper treatment and gorgeous carpeting. When the wallpaper pattern is as complex as this one, it's advisable to tone down the other patterns in the room. The fabric of the sofa matches the wallpaper exactly, while the carpet, chair, and ottoman are all treated to much more subtle designs. An awe-inspiring domed ceiling with an ornate lighting fixture contributes to the formal theme.*

ABOVE: *Subtle decorative effects like the soothing blue walls and white-painted fireplace mantel impart a sense of calm, creating the perfect backdrop for a comfortable corner in which to relax. Outfitted with a wonderful divan and select Victorian accessories, it's a picture-perfect setting.*

RIGHT: *Walls decorated in three distinct horizontal sections—a treatment known as the tripartite wall—were the darlings of the Gilded Age. Here, a wall-papered dado covers the bottom portion of the wall, while the midsection, or field, is painted. The beautiful wallpaper frieze at the top of the wall gives way to a color-coordinated, papered ceiling. Tripartite wall treatments were in vogue during the 1870s and 1880s, and are a popular choice for today's formal Victorian interiors.*

LEFT: *An under-eaves bedroom has been made all the more inviting by papering the ceiling as well as the walls. This technique unifies the irregular space, creating a cozy nook for over-night guests. A mini-print such as this is an especially popular choice for the tiny, Victorian-inspired bedroom—splashy florals or large geometrics would make a small space seem claustrophobic. Above the window, a decorative cornice harbors a sumptuous fabric shade in a treatment that provides both privacy and a pulled-together look.*

OPPOSITE: *Victorian elegance can be found in the beautiful craftsmanship and warm, honey colors of this staircase and hardwood floor. The strong, clean lines of the staircase recall the emphasis placed on quality and simplicity by the proponents of the Arts and Crafts Movement. A lovely Oriental rug dresses the floor with a notable touch of pattern and texture, protecting the wood even as it provides softness underfoot.*

OPPOSITE: *In this formal Victorian bath a stunning wall treatment becomes the center of attention. Beautiful tilework ornamented with a floral bouquet is topped by a wall that has been ragged a soft green. At the wall's top, a border continues the floral theme. The tile floor, too, has been treated to a design that picks up the green of the walls and incorporates the delicate florals used in the wall tiles and border. Framed botanical prints and fresh flowers at the pedestal sink provide the perfect decorative touch.*

RIGHT: *Special effects can create dramatic impact. This appealing bath is made all the more beautiful with a customized wall treatment. Painted stripes above the wall molding correspond to the colors used in the diamond pattern painted on bead-board paneling below. The sunny, nature-inspired colors are repeated in the decorative accessories, and the overall theme is one of slightly eccentric Victorian charm.*

LEFT: *A layered window dressing complete with an undercurtain, drapes, valance, and swag is quintessential Victorian style. Details such as the tiny tassels, fringe, and braiding in the valance and swag add formal flair, while the yellow checked undercurtain tempers the romantic floral of the wallpaper.*

ABOVE: *A beamed ceiling and decorative cornice draw the eye upward in this well-appointed room. These elements effectively divide the ceiling into sections, adding depth, visual interest, and architectural embellishment. Note too, how the rich pomegranate color of the walls, coupled with deep green accents and the stark white of mantel and ceiling, lend dramatic impact in a formal setting.*

RIGHT: *A breath-taking chandelier presides over the dining room table, creating instant elegance. Walls painted a creamy fawn are endowed with a decorative— and functional— chair rail in a clear white. A handsome fireplace and detailed cornice complete the backdrop for this formal Victorian dining room.*

BELOW: *Reminiscent of the mid-Victorian period, this room has been treated to a singular wallpaper pattern and a simple but elegant cornice that defines the decorative, painted tin ceiling. The polished hardwood floor is accented with decorative area rugs, and a lovely brass chandelier hangs above the center table.*

ABOVE: *A delicate fabric shade offers additional privacy and a filter for sunlight when lace curtains are the window treatment of choice. Here, a lace panel and a filmy white curtain are tied back with an elegant cord and tassel that makes a beautiful statement in this formal room. This lovely window dressing softens the richness of the gilt mirror and marble-top table.*

ABOVE: *Formal Victorian spirit is clearly conveyed in these luxurious window treatments. French doors at the left are dressed in sheers and layered with a rich drapery topped by a scalloped and tasseled valance. The window on the right is treated in similar fashion, but boasts an Austrian shade as an undercurtain, or "glass curtain," as the Victorians called it. Wallpaper in a rich gold color echoes the sumptuous hue of the draperies.*

CHAPTER FOUR

FURNISHING WITH ELEGANCE

Today's Victorian Revival in interior design allows us to choose from a variety of nineteenth-century styles in outfitting the elegant interior. Antique pieces are still available and reproductions are being created by well-known furniture manufacturers. Vintage furnishings can also be updated with modern fabrics, and pieces can be used in a variety of imaginative ways.

Furnishings for a formal Victorian decor are typically made of rich hardwoods such as mahogany, cherry, walnut, or rosewood. In addition, there are beautiful oaks with light or dark stains, fanciful wicker, bamboo, and even artistic metal pieces, which were popular on the porch and in the garden or sunroom.

The formal Victorian parlor or living room can be handsomely dressed with a matching suite including a sofa or settee, gentleman's chair, lady's chair, and side chairs. If matched pieces aren't available to you or simply don't suit your tastes, choice pieces that display the characteristics of various nineteenth-century styles can be combined with smashing results. Plush, upholstered sofas can be mixed with comfortable easy chairs sporting traditional fabrics. Consider rich fabrics to impart a formal tone: velvet, satin, damask, and brocade are ideal for achieving an elegant effect.

A round center table can become a focal point in the well-appointed parlor or furnishings can be arranged in symmetrical fashion, with side tables situated near seating. Additional pieces such as bookcases or secretaries, ottomans and footstools, musical instruments, or an étagère (a freestanding piece with decorative shelves used to display a collection or bric-a-brac) further enhance the formal Victorian spirit.

Dining rooms, whether large or small, can be elegantly dressed with a matching table and chairs and a sideboard. China cabinets are also ideal in this setting.

Bedrooms lavishly furnished with an impressive wooden bed, dresser, and chest of drawers can convey high style Victorian spirit, but a beautifully ornate brass or iron bed can achieve the same results.

Kitchens full of glass-front cabinetry or cupboards in rich wood tones recall the elegance of days gone by. Often, by adding a singular piece such as an exquisite freestanding cupboard, a touch of formal Victorian spirit can be easily summoned.

Whichever room you wish to focus on—or perhaps you'll decorate them all—the Victorian era offers dozens of examples of beautifully designed furniture styles, all perfect for creating a formal atmosphere.

OPPOSITE: *An area of this handsome Victorian bedroom is given over to comfortable relaxation. A tasteful divan, upholstered rocking chair, and balloon-back armchair with matching footstool close by the fireplace afford ample seating for moments of quiet. The beautiful gilt mirror outfits the dressing table and reflects a massive four-poster bed.*

ABOVE: *The front porch is the ideal location for light and airy wicker furnishings. Here, a selection of styles blends admirably to create an alfresco dining area that works in combination with a sitting area. While vintage pieces were routinely used outdoors, not all reproductions are weather-resistant. Check to be sure new wicker pieces can withstand the elements.*

RIGHT: *A selection of Victorian-inspired furnishings has been beautifully upholstered in a fabric that matches the floral wallpaper. The molded iron divan was probably originally a porch fixture, but with the addition of a cushion and several pillows it becomes a piece worthy of any parlor. Lushly upholstered armchairs with dark wood trim, which were a favorite of the Victorians, here bolster the formality of the space. An oversized ottoman serving as coffee table adds an exotic note. The overall effect is stunning and romantic, proving that "formal" does not have to imply "restrained."*

RIGHT: *Oriental influence moves center stage in an artistic vignette that features a handsome bamboo table. The exotic theme is continued in the decorative fabric screen behind the table, beautifully framed artwork, and a collection of blue and white china.*

BELOW: *Many nineteenth-century sitting rooms were organized around a center table, upon which games were played, books were stacked, or sewing accoutrements rested. The ample center table here is surrounded by a selection of comfortable armchairs, in true Victorian fashion. A blue velvet lady's chair—so called because it was designed for women, whose voluminous skirts could not be comfortably accommodated in an armchair—is situated close to the warmth of the fire. An opulent mirror with shelves for figurines, an easel for displaying artwork, and an elegant footstool contribute to the formal scheme in this inviting room.*

ABOVE: *Classic elegance echoes through this room, thanks to a beautifully accessorized divan. The flowing lines of the mahogany piece create a sense of serenity, while gilded, applied designs dress up the inherently casual nature of the divan; a marble-top gilt table and a richly upholstered armchair are perfect accompaniments. Formal, yet inviting and comfortable, this setting is proof positive that Victorian fashions can aptly meet the needs of today's busy lifestyles.*

BELOW: *Accomplished men and women of the Victorian era prided themselves on the ability to play a musical instrument. Pianos were commonly found in the homes of the well-to-do and are a wonderful addition to today's formal Victorian interior. With a selection of sheet music and a potpourri of decorative items to dress the piano top, this pretty corner could easily be the focal point of the room.*

LEFT: *This Rococo Revival settee incorporates the delicate but ornate carvings typical of the French-derived style. Embellishments such as flowers, tendrils, and scrolls commonly adorned the arms, legs, and backs of Rococo Revival furniture, which was generally crafted of black walnut or rosewood. Buttoned and tufted velvet adds to the richness of this piece, which makes a perfect perch for a tea party.*

RIGHT: *Aesthetic sensibilities and a salute to the exotic are evident in this eye-catching corner, where a bamboo cupboard takes center stage. In true Victorian fashion, artifacts of nature are brought indoors and the motifs on wallpaper, china, and other accessories celebrate the beauty of the natural world. Starfish and seashells line the shelves of the cabinet, peacock feathers adorn a figurine of the bird, and a wallpaper with Oriental influence provides the perfect backdrop for this nature-inspired vignette.*

RIGHT: *This formal dining room is well out-fitted with matching wood-rimmed, upholstered chairs, a gleaming wood table, and a commodious china cabinet. Scroll and modified shell designs were popular ornaments on wooden pieces during the nineteenth century, and many such designs can be found today, although a vintage matched set would be a rare discovery indeed. Many companies are now producing furniture in traditional Victorian designs, and these reproductions offer the best hope for creating a dining room steeped in the formality of the Gilded Age.*

ABOVE: *A majestic four poster dominates this refined bedroom. The beautifully turned posts are capped by classic finials, accenting the formality of the piece. Blanket chests traditionally rested at the foot of the bed, where an extra quilt was close at hand if the night turned unexpectedly chilly. A handsome chest of drawers, with integrated posts that match those of the bed, completes the set. This arrangement was typical of the bedrooms of the nineteenth century and works just as well for us today.*

BELOW: *An eclectic dining room blends pressed-back Victorian chairs with an oval table and a rugged sideboard. The mixing of various furniture styles was de rigueur in the late-nineteenth-century home as new style emerged and old ones faded. Most families couldn't afford to indulge in an entirely new set of furniture with every trend; instead they invested in one or two stylish pieces and combined these with older pieces they already owned. This eclectic look was a mainstay of Victorian homes and continues to be popular into the nineties.*

ABOVE: *This simple china cupboard gains a touch of decoration with a row of Gothic arches parading across the top of glass doors. Filled to overflow with pretty teapots, cups, and desert plates, the piece is both beautiful and functional, as it protects the china from dust and breakage. Subtle details, such as the lace doilies that adorn the shelves and the tassel tied to the key, contribute to the formal effect.*

BELOW: *A marble-top table with an ornate iron base provides a place for informal meals in a tiny apartment kitchen. The space allows for an old-fashioned Hoosier cupboard, which was used to store dry goods and dishware, and served as a counter and baking area. Ideal for extra storage, Hoosier cupboards have become increasingly popular as collectors and decorators began to appreciate the charm and practicality of the pieces. Note too, the glass-front cabinetry above the sink and the period perfect tile floor.*

ABOVE: *Smaller spaces and scaled-down furnishings can have big impact. This intimate dining area is outfitted with a round table and elegant chairs with upholstered seats. Little else is called for given the romantic setting: a beautiful Victorian wall treatment, lavish window dressing, formal chandelier, and rich table setting bestow maximum Victorian effect even without additional furniture.*

ABOVE: *In the late 1800s, wooden beds fell out of favor, and brass or iron beds, which were thought to be more sanitary, took their place. This ornate iron bed has brass detailing, a combination that became very popular in the 1890s. With the addition of a comfortable easy chair for good measure, a painted bedside table, and long-cherished possessions you've got the ideal Victorian-inspired retreat.*

BELOW: *Intellectual pursuits and an appreciation of fine music are conveyed via the furnishings in this high style parlor. A handsome combination bookcase-secretary (the center panel folds down into a desk) indicates the premium placed on education by the Victorians. Musical accomplishment, too, was admired, and a heavily carved piano bears witness to the importance given to music appreciation. Chairs upholstered in rich velvets soften the serious intent of bookcase and piano, inviting readers (or listeners) to sit back and relax in style. The overall effect is refined yet spirited.*

ABOVE: *Fit for a robber baron, this ornate half-tester bed (with canopy extending over the head of the bed only) repeats the elegant fabric found in the elaborate window dressing. An exquisite Rococo Revival–style armchair sits before the window on the right.*

A B O V E : *Natural elements are the focus of this inviting dining room.*
The deep wood tones of the furniture, including the elegant sideboard, are
complemented by the lighter color of the polished hardwood floor. Furnish-
ings and accessories are kept to a minimum, while the walls and moldings
subtly impart formal Victorian spirit.

LEFT: *This formal Victorian living room is beautifully furnished with a suite of Rococo Revival-style pieces. The elegant rosewood settee and matching armchairs are upholstered in a soft fabric bedecked with floral sprays; the serpentine back of the settee and carved flowers on the pieces are classic features of Rococo Revival designs. Embellished with gilt Egyptian-style designs, the stunning center table sports a beautiful top of imported marble. Here, the seating is grouped for intimate conversation, rather than in a more formal, symmetrical arrangement.*

BELOW: *Home comforts and an inviting table recall the Victorian penchant for entertaining. Elegantly dressed with a handsome table, chairs, and sideboard, this lovely dining room offers timeless appeal. A family portrait holds a place of honor above the fireplace and a beautiful floral wallpaper contributes to the old-fashioned air of the room.*

RIGHT: *This Victorian pantry is elegant as well as functional thanks to beautiful glass-front cabinetry. Gleaming woodwork, a tile floor, and a decorative backsplash are notable nineteenth-century elements. Attractive enough to admit guests, the room is a perfect buffet serving space, with the countertop serving as an extensive sideboard.*

BELOW: *Tea for two is on the menu in this beautiful Victorian sitting room. Rococo Revival-style chairs, upholstered in traditional dark-colored damask, are pulled up to an elegant table set close to the hearth. A period secretary in the corner is the ideal spot for dashing off notes to friends or paying bills. Vintage furnishings are highlighted by tastefully wallpapered walls and the beautiful area rug.*

ABOVE: *Often even a single piece of furniture can have dramatic impact when decorating in the Victorian style. This beautiful armoire with applied moldings and carved ornamentation elegantly stands alone against a lovely wallpapered background. Because Victorian rooms were not generally equipped with closets, the wardrobe was an essential piece, and many bedrooms housed more than one.*

ABOVE: *Oftentimes, a wonderful relic from the past can be put to work in the present day. In this bath, a nineteenth-century commode-washstand has been adapted to house a modern sink basin. Also note the beautiful old sewing machine that now serves as a dressing table. Ingenuity combined with period-perfect decorative details creates stunning results.*

CHAPTER FIVE
TRADITIONAL TOUCHES

Last but far from least, creating a formal Victorian interior calls for special touches that accessorize your room and add a highly personal note. Your color preferences are reflected throughout your interior and your taste is expressed in the furnishings you select. Your interests, passions, and character, however, are conveyed through the items you choose to display throughout your rooms—objects that bring warmth and personality to your Victorian home.

Elegant nineteenth-century rooms were filled with accessories of glass, porcelain, brass, or silver—time-honored materials rich in detail. Decorative touches such as fringed or tasseled pillows, fresh flowers, crisp linens, and gilt or sterling picture frames contribute fabulous color and texture. Books, whether placed on a tabletop or lined on a series of shelves become old friends we can't live without.

Dining room tables are works of art when set with special china and cutlery, and walls throughout your home can reflect your creative sensibilities by showcasing paintings and drawings. Cherished mementos are ideal for arranging eye-catching vignettes on tabletops, while fireplace mantels and built-in shelves, are perfect for displaying collections.

Bringing nature indoors, which speaks volumes about your interests, and was a favorite decorating tip of Victorian women; a collection of shells, an arrangement of dried flowers, or even garden accessories such as old urns can be an enchanting touch in a traditional setting.

Antiques shops and shows offer wonderful possibilities for acquiring beautiful relics from the Victorian past. Often, developing a working relationship with a dealer specializing in your particular interests is an excellent way to build a collection. Invest in quality rather than quantity to assure treasures you'll be pleased with for years to come.

Contemporary items, such as fine china, crystal, or porcelain are available through better department stores and fine gift shops. Don't forget to explore art galleries and auctions for artwork and decorative accessories.

Whether your tastes run to peacock feathers and seashells or to fine china and silver candlesticks, there is room for your treasures in your formal Victorian home. This is the opportunity to personalize your home with the things you love, all the while adding the finishing touches to a gracious and comfortable interior.

OPPOSITE: *The Victorians greatly admired exquisite penmanship, and during the nineteenth century books on ornamental lettering, along with the accoutrements of letter writing, became highly fashionable. A silver ink stand with cut crystal ink bottles celebrates the art of letter writing, and fine silver candlesticks and an exotic quill pen add traditional elements to this charming vignette.*

LEFT: *A well-dressed table is largely a matter of personal choice. Here, colorful china, gilt-trimmed stemware, and polished silver join decorative sterling candlesticks atop an elegant tablecloth. During the nineteenth century, new machinery made lace affordable as never before. Victorian women bought lengths of lace and sewed it to table linens to create their own heirloom pieces.*

ABOVE: *Traditional touches such as tassels, braiding, and fringe make these pillows a most welcome addition to any seat in the house. Formal elegance is evoked with rich, subtly patterned fabrics and glorious attention to detail.*

RIGHT: *An artistic glass-front cupboard is perfect for displaying a collection of small ceramic figures and assorted items. Tall brass candlesticks, a gilt mirror, and whimsical cherubs add an elegant touch to this visual feast.*

BELOW: *An Oriental theme is apparent in the Japanese folding screen and Japanesque ceramic lamp, but the motif is tempered by a European sterling silver tea service. Such combinations of Oriental designs with traditional American or European pieces were a favorite of Victorians—this juxtaposition demonstrated to guests a love of travel and an appreciation of the exotic, even while the family remained firmly grounded in Western culture.*

ABOVE: *Whether in the library or covering a wall in the parlor, built-in bookshelves are ideal for displaying treasured books. Here, a small table joins the setting to exhibit an array of wooden candlesticks and cherished photos.*

RIGHT: *Tabletop vignettes gave the Victorians a way to enjoy the beauty of the objects around them. These charming still lifes often incorporated family photographs, decorative boxes, stacks of favorite books, and even polished stones or seashells. This delightful vignette combines fresh flowers, a traditional lamp, and a beautiful hand-painted plate that echoes the colors and floral pattern in the romantic drapes.*

BELOW: *Pretty as a picture, elegant china, a bouquet of roses, and delicate linen napkins bring a measure of elegance to the great outdoors. After-noon coffee on the terrace is enjoyed all the more thanks to this lovely service.*

ABOVE: *Mother Nature is much admired in this tabletop display of favorite items. A black-and-white print is accompanied by an ivy topiary, a care-worn pitcher that holds collected candles, a tiny bird's nest, and a simple pottery vase with a single bright bloom. Gardening books are close at hand and contribute to the nature-inspired theme of this peaceful setting.*

ABOVE: *No corner was left untouched in the proper Victorian home, and this lovely corner has it all. A beautifully arranged tabletop vignette spotlights a highly ornamented clock, family photos with ornate frames, fresh flowers, and an unusual antique lamp, while a plush needlepoint pillow accessorizes the sofa.*

BELOW: *A mantel or special shelf is the ideal location for a cherished object. This magnificent clock of painted wood easily stands alone and speaks volumes with regard to the type of traditional touches that enhance a Victorian setting.*

OPPOSITE: *Beautiful oil paintings and framed prints turn this corner of a Victorian bedroom into a miniature art gallery. Crisp white walls and bedding, as well as simple furnishings, allow artwork to take center stage. A small stack of books and a lamp base fashioned from a Japanesque vase reinforce the aura of culture that resonates from the small space.*

ABOVE: *This airy conservatory plays host to an abundance of flowering plants and greenery arranged in antique wirework plant stands, which were popular during the late nineteenth century. A medley of furnishings is juxtaposed with an elegant table setting for a casual yet refined effect.*

LEFT: *Natural elegance results from placing a collection of antique glass bottles—mainly medicine bottles—on a gilt-trimmed tray. Even if traditional antique accessories are out of your budget, the everyday objects of yesteryear possess a charm that translates well in a modern setting, and they're available at a fraction of the cost of crystal, fine china, or silver. Another nontraditional touch—a favorite piece of artwork hangs in the window rather than on a wall. The effect is simple yet stunning, demonstrating that high style doesn't have to be high cost.*

LEFT: *Candlelight and roses—was there ever a more beautiful combination? A hall table is the setting for this alluring and artless bouquet. Light from two candles—set in opulent candlesticks trimmed with dangling prisms—is reflected in the gilt mirror, thereby doubling the amount of light. This arrangement not only conveys Victorian splendor, but is a wonderful way to say welcome.*

OPPOSITE: *Formal restraint is apparent in this elegant room, where favorite objects fuse with lovely furnishings to create a parlor with subtle charm. The table beside the wing chair includes a selection of vibrantly colored glassware; the mantel displays additional cherished objects, including a figurine and a decorative plate. Opulent touches are found in the fringed ottoman, sumptuous throw pillow, and framed artwork.*

BELOW: *Vintage garden tools seem right at home alongside a beautiful piece of sculpture and an artistic jardiniere planted with wildflowers. Here, a creative touch and passion for gardening results in a beautiful and highly personal display.*

ABOVE: *Breakfast is served in this beautiful Victorian bedroom. An old-fashioned tray table boasts a rose-sprigged breakfast setting, complete with an egg cup and a miniature teapot. Beyond the tray, a skirted dressing table is accessorized with a sterling silver dresser set, delicate rose buds, and silver-lidded glass jars.*

RIGHT: *The intricate details and domed top of a Victorian wirework birdcage serves as an architectural embellishment in this graceful setting. Positioned in front of a sunny window, the cage casts its ethereal shadow on an expanse of wall. The framed poster depicts birds in flight, continuing the ornithological theme of this serene corner.*

BELOW: *Vintage periodicals offer a fascinating glimpse into the manners and morals of an age, and endow your rooms with a sense of history. The Craftsman, founded by furniture designer Gustave Stickley, embraced the ideals of the Arts and Crafts Movement, which encouraged sturdy construction and simple design.*

ABOVE: *Cast-iron furniture—in Victorian times used almost exclusively in the garden—now finds a home indoors as well. As the nineteenth century advanced, designs grew ever more ornate, with vines, acanthus leaves, ferns, grape clusters, and birds among the most popular motifs. Consider adding a cast-iron piece to your Victorian interior for an unusual yet traditional touch.*

RIGHT: *Nearly every family boasts at least one antique souvenir left from a great-uncle's European tour or a great-grandmother's wedding trip. The Victorians were passionate about travel, and the trifles they brought back can be incorporated into your decor. Here, a set of miniature prints of world landmarks collected and set in circular frames provides an interesting counterpoint to old family photographs and vintage iron toys.*